O Frabjous Day!

O Frabjous Day!

A Selection of Poems: 2019-2023

by Don Gutteridge

Selection and Introduction by
Brian T. W. Way

For Sue
with love & fond
memories —
Don

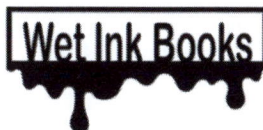

Wet Ink Books

First Edition

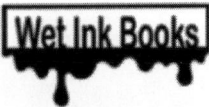

Wet Ink Books
www.WetInkBooks.com
WetInkBooks@gmail.com

O Frabjous Day!
by Don Gutteridge

Selection and Introduction by Brian T. W. Way
Cover Design – Richard M. Grove
Layout and Design – Richard M. Grove
Cover Image Info – Wonderland bunny with design elements
by Pushkin - courtesy of Shutterstock - used by permission

Typeset in Garamond
Printed and bound in Canada
Distributed in USA by Ingram,
    – to set up an account – 1-800-937-0152

Library and Archives Canada Cataloguing in Publication

Title: O frabjous day! : a selection of poems, 2019-2023 / by Don Gutteridge ; selection and introduction by Brian T. W. Way.
Other titles: Poems. Selections (2023 : Wet Ink Books)
Names: Gutteridge, Don, 1937- author. |
Way, Brian T. W. (Brian Thomas Wesley), 1951- editor.
Identifiers: Canadiana 20230191509 | ISBN 9781989786871 (softcover)
Classification: LCC PS8513.U85 A6 2023 | DDC C811/.54—dc23

To Don

Table of Contents

from:
A Ground More Arable

from:
Masters of the Craft

We shall not cease from exploration
And the end of all our exploring
Will be to arrive where we started
And know the place for the first time.

—T. S. Eliot "Little Gidding" *Four Quartets*

The Walrus and the Carpenter
Walked on a mile or so,
And then they rested on a rock
Conveniently low:
And all the little Oysters stood
And waited in a row.

"The time has come," the Walrus said,
"To talk of many things:
Of shoes—and ships—and sealing-wax—
Of cabbages—and kings—
And why the sea is boiling hot—
And whether pigs have wings."

—Lewis Carroll *Through the Looking-Glass*

# of mirror and memory

Just after Alice slips through the mirror in Chapter One of *Through the Looking-Glass*, she finds an unusual book which is, as she says, "all in some language I don't know." But quickly, she realizes "Why, it's a Looking-glass book, of course!" and promptly holds the book up to a mirror where letters and words are reversed, deciphered; then, in this mirror-within-a-mirror (a dichotomy that extends throughout the novel), Alice reads a poem entitled "Jabberwocky"—generally acclaimed as one of the greatest nonsense poems in English literature, here, serving as an introduction to Alice's riddle-filled trip through Looking-Glass Land (the quixotic world of reversals that resides behind the hearth-mirror in her family's Victorian living room). Alice's critical analysis of the poem is characteristically honest though limited, the crystal-clear view of a child: "It seems very pretty, but it's *rather* hard to understand. ... Somehow it seems to fill my head with ideas—only I don't exactly know what they are." In essence, "Jabberwocky" is a playful celebration of language, of words that are often not words, a parodic narrative poem composed with an inventive, sometimes meaningless lexis, as much sight and sound as sense, nevertheless telling the tale of a mythic quest by a son to slay a terrible monster, the Jabberwock. The quest is successful and, with the creature's decapitated head, the son returns to the delight of his parent: "Come to my arms, my beamish boy! / O frabjous day! Callooh! Callay!" Then, "curiouser and curiouser" and reminiscent of almost every horror story's final scene, the poem ends with an exact repetition of the first stanza, hinting that the quest may not quite be over after all; it seems about to begin again, and again—like all quests, perhaps, like a child growing up in a book?

In Looking-Glass Land, any resolution or meaning exists only in reflected reversal, in the exigent games and puzzles encountered inside Alice's enigmatic dichotomy of mirrors—the book is a game of chess, after all, a game of mirrors. And of course, for millennia, after streams, reflection in mirrors was a primary source of self-awareness for humans, from pure insight to pure narcissism, now cast in Selfies, Facetime, Skype and the rest.

O Frabjous Day! is a representative selection of the poetry published by Don Gutteridge between 2019 and 2023. Of course, all poets weave their craft with many threads; they may fabricate their work as sonnets or odes, as epics or haiku, colour it with complex tropes and motifs, or leave it sparse and unadorned as a barren wasteland; and even beyond that, all works fashion a voice unique to the writer and to the moment. Don Gutteridge's poems as presented in *O Frabjous Day!* are no exception. While any generalization about artistic execution is invariably fraught with peril, at the very least here Gutteridge's poems strive toward a distinctive poetic, with a dualism not unlike Alice's mirror-world, reflecting eras present and past, with a voice both adult and child, in a place both here and there—fixed in time and timeless. Frequently expressing an ornate versification that captures the feel of a childhood lived in the nineteen-thirties and forties, and often representing that time with a guileless, child-like sensibility—unusual interests and observations, stylized diction and commonplace topics, euphemisms both innocent and comic (there is a lot of wit and humour in these pages)—the poems, nonetheless, are expressed through the lean nuance of a contemporary, adult perception—one thinks, at times, of that distanced, experienced view of Blake as he delivers his "Songs of Innocence" or, perhaps, of Emily Dickinson who always seems standing just a bit apart, looking over a shoulder as her poetic persona speaks (as indeed she lived slightly apart in her domestic sanctuary in Amherst). A specific range of traditional literary tropes is used by Gutteridge, particularly alliteration ("...the moon endeavors to gild / the gloaming with its glistened glow..." or "as cozy as a cocoon, cradling / a chrysalis..."), internal rhyme ("... I want to follow her / down, and drown" or

"…for anything other / than doing and dying" or "O to be that boy again! / to befuddle in puddles the rain"), and supplemental prefixes, sometimes hyphenated ("anew" "a-lurk" "a-bob" "adream" "a-whee" "abed" "un-venomed" "unpoppied" "unabide" "un-lunged"). Overall, the predominant scheme utilised is prosaic, many poems essentially a declarative sentence focussed on a particular topic or memory and then creatively embroidered as the poet sees fit, with line breaks that seem selvedged more by happenstance than by determined breath-stops or dramatic pauses. Like the sparse works of Dickinson or Jay Macpherson, Gutteridge's poems are often simply wrought but dramatically charged with subtle intensity and layered meanings.

Thematically, several poems in *O Frabjous Day!* deal with the grief of sorrow, meditations on the passing of the poet's wife, Anne, and his grandson, Tom, and attempting to find some manner to ease and to cope with the illimitable pain of such loss. As that pain is deep, in that vein, one realizes that many of the works here are love poems, love for family, for memories, for place, for poetry itself. And several poems contemplate religion and the nature of God often with a sceptic's tone (a thematic attitude common in much of Gutteridge's prose fiction, as well) but most of these writings offer reflections on growing up in Point Edward, remembering childhood friends, neighbours, and caregivers and recalling experiences around the village and along the shores of the St. Clair River and Lake Huron, on the sands of Canatara. Specifically, many poems deal in one way or another with coming-of-age where puberty and sexual awakening begin to intercede among teen-agers and relationships take on new directions. As part of that life cycle, many poems also contemplate the changing perception of parents and grandparents, brother, aunt and uncle, all part of the poet's growing-up and maturation. Anthropomorphically, place becomes a living presence in these poems, the enchanting lure of the village's streets and the nearby waters becoming a kind of caregiver in itself, protective chaperon both through the early journey of the poet's life and in the adult's remembrance of things past:

These dunes, older
than Methuselah's dam,
lie adrift in their own sleep,
crowned with sea-grasses
that weep in the on-shore
breeze...

And in that, Gutteridge joins a vast company of Canadian writers and artists, finding a vital life-force in his own backyard— from sea to sea, the likes of Moodie, Grove, Roy, Buckler, Leacock, Ross, Richler, Marlatt, Laurence, Purdy, Birney, Suknaski, Reaney, Garner, Kroetsche, Munro, J. B. Lee, Atwood, and many others—so much so, such writing begins to feel like a Canadian thing, an intrinsic part of our literary identity! And to a great degree, these writers only achieved success as writers when they found that wellspring nearby; like that essential Algoma landscape that became the dynamic filter for the Group of Seven, the Point Edward locale is a muscular and influential muse throughout Gutteridge's work:

and I was now arrived:
a circumnavigator
like Magellan or Drake, gallivanting
the globe—only to find
the home we never leave

A note about alliteration which overtly enhances and empowers so many of these poems. As a trope, of course, it has a long history in various literatures and cultures. As a rhythmic device, alliteration tends to slow down one's reading of a work (just try reading a 'tongue twister' quickly), and thus boldly places an emphasis on certain words, phrases and ideas. It compels reflection and slow time and fits the poems of *O Frabjous Day!* like a surgical glove. Alliteration can be found in the proverbial Sanskrit Shlokas and in the early literary works of the Norse, Germanic, Saxon, Gaeilge and

Anglish. It is the predominant style of the Old English *Beowulf* ("Oft Scyld Scefing sceaþena þreatum, / monegum mægþum, meodosetla ofteah, / egsode eorlas") and the Middle Ages' *Sir Gawain and the Green Knight*: "Siþen þe sege & þe assaut watȝ sesed at Troye, / Þe borȝ brittened & brent to brondeȝ & askeȝ ..." And in contemporary time, it is a common device in advertising and product marketing: *Don't Dream it; Drive it; Maybe it's Maybelline; What's in your Wallet; Krispy Kreme; Coca Cola; Best Buy*. But its use in contemporary poetry has pretty much disappeared. While the best Victorian poets—Tennyson, Browning, Arnold, Swinburne, Longfellow, and the Rossettis (Wordsworth, too)—were exacting and brilliant in their manipulation of prosody, of rhythmic schemes and rhyme, late in the age, Gerard Manley Hopkins, in a series of letters (circa 1880), espoused his idea of "sprung rhythm" as a theory to shape his poetry and make it sound more natural and realistic—to put an end to the triviality inherent in the overuse of galloping rhythms and artificial devices to which so much Victorian poetry had sunk. This kind of thinking led to the Modernist dismissal of ornate versification, the rise of *vers libre*, and as philosopher T. E. Hulme predicted, the coming of a period of "dry, hard, classical verse" (*Speculations*). In the steps of Modernists like Eliot, Pound, williams, Auden and Stevens, followed by the Beat, Confessional, Black Mountain and Counterculture writers like Ginsberg, Plath, Lowell, Purdy, Olson, Snyder and Roethke, poets used few devices beyond precise diction, image, metaphor or symbol. Here, in *O Frabjous Day!,* Gutteridge re-infuses his poetry with alliteration as a traditional and arcane device—in a verse that often reaches back in time for its inspiration, the method also reaches back to retrieve and reuse this lost trope. In a prosy yet sparse poetic, he writes his life with wit, poignancy, bemusement, insight and bewilderment frequently intertwining his lines alliteratively, as he might claim, with "bardic bravado." The result is in your hands to construe how you may. Be mindful, of course, with any artistic manifestation no interpretation can ever really be absolute, yours or mine, especially in the ever-swirling vortex of time; there is always some mystery or potential for redirection at the core, for the reader and, very often, for the writer, too. We rarely see all that mirrors reflect, or understand entire what memories contain. When Polonius asks, "What do you read, my lord?", Hamlet's evasive but insightful response is "Words, words, words." Unlike the deadly vorpal blade, the signification of words, no matter how precise *or* nonsensical, is often an equivocal thing, words as slippery as those "behemoth bass" the poet angles for in Cameron Lake, as evasive as the slithy, brillig words of "Jabberwocky," as peculiarly compelling as the quest itself. So, read and enjoy these poems; read and enjoy, and in the end, at the very least simply say, "O frabjous day!"

—Brian T. W. Way

from:

More Boding than Blood

More Boding than Blood

For Tom in loving memory

If you had lived but one
more day, I would have walked you
into the milkweed meadow
where butterflies unbutton
their wings to bask on the breeze
and puckered pods, lanced
by light, expose their silken
sofas and larks sweeten
the air with saccharine song
and grasshoppers fling
free of gravity on tiny
trapezes and puff-adders
sputter loud enough
to frighten the frogs holidaying
on the pond and bulrushes
fluff their rusted coiffures—
and you would have said,
"So this is where the poems
gave birth to themselves?"
and I would reply, "Here
and in the kind of love
you brought me, more boding
than blood, more basic
than bone."

Remembrance

In the Point we called our cenotaph
simply "The Monument," and etched
in stolid stone were the names
of long-ago battles
too brutal to be celebrated,
and on the slim plinth
a roll-call of those
who gave their all for the king
of a far country, and atop
this edifice of remembrance
the bust of an unknown soldier
stares out over the town,
looking lonely and unanointed.

Beyond Hope

If there were a god dispensing
kudos and brickbats,
I could curse him for letting Tom die,
but I am not a man
of belief in matters beyond
hope, and so my grief
must bleed leeward to brood
in the bone, and my cries for relief
find no home,
here or in Heaven.

Ode

In my town poems grew
on trees like apples from the orchards
of Eden, nurtured by a consenting
sun and ripe for plucking
by the first apprentice bard
to feel the surge of a word
he couldn't define or a rhythm
needing a rhyme to capture
a cadence, and I felt blessed
to be a budding balladeer
among my people and tuck
their hopes and happiness in the
throes of an ode.

Blinding

Missus Bradley wandered
her clapboard abode,
wondering what room
she was in, and when nothing
came to mind, stood
staring from her front stoop
under a sun that bloomed
too blinding for the eye
and, her thoughts thickening,
wondered what'd happened
to the sky.

Autumn Morning: 1960

Whenever I feel the need
to ease the grip of my grief,
I dream of that October
morning when you pulled up
to the curb in your sleek Beetle
and stepped out like Cleopatra
debouching from her barge,
the breeze making a halo
of your hair, your lips a limned
ellipse, your eyes as lively
as agates in a toddler's palm
and as blue as the sky is deep,
and I knew for the first time
that a smile could calm the churning
chambers of a heart—and such
a remembrance, for a moment,
soothes a bereavement pain
that stings like a cinder smouldering
in the bone.

Delirium

O Tom! There is no
pain like the kind that fractures
my heart whenever I think
of you unalive, somewhere
without the lithium of light
or the salve of love's solace,
and my grief breaks over me
like a tidal tantrum loosed
by the moon in oscillating
inundations, and anywhere
I turn I see your adoring
eyes and I know it's just
the delirium of dream, but I
prize it just the same
and let it stoke the wokened
locus of my loss, for when
you died, you left me bitter
in the bone, like a body embalmed.

A Kind of Joy

In the midst of my grief, the thought
of your elfin grin blooms
in my mind, and soothes, and a
kind of joy wells up
when I remember I had you
whole and aloft for thirty
years and more, and we kept
room in our hearts for a love
beyond the reach of belief,
and O my beautiful boy!
you have settled softly into my soul.

Autumnal Wind

When the wind hums autumnal,
Earth denies the dying:
leaves forgo their green
sheen for a crimson ignition
and melons mellow in the fields,
plumped by the last licks
of a lapsing sun, and butternut
seethes with seed and robins
fatten and feather in time
for their continental cruise
and orchards hang heavy
with newly juiced fruit
and roses doze like dowagers
in final flourish, and all
things natural, however
hard they may have tried,
like you, were unprepared
to die.

All the Days

I loved you most in the morning
when sunlight gilded the grass
and dappled the dew, and a breeze,
derelict from the dawn, breathed
easy in the maples and rippled
the face of the Lake like shook silk
and a robin's song throbbed
in his throat—
and I loved you most in the afternoon
when the sun snoozed in a high
sky and breezes blew
as if they mattered and larks
sent their serenades meandering
over meadows, and rollers,
freshening in the Lake, consoled
the nearest shore—
and I loved you most in the evening
when the breeze subtled and the moon
marinated the stars and induced
a drifting of dream, and children
played hide-and-seek,
charmed by the dark—
I loved you then and all
the days before, and even
though you've gone, I love you
even more.

from:

The Ardent Dark

Bugle

Long ago, when the Earth
had too many moons,
the Attawandaron came
to Canatara to take
the waters, gather clams
and worship their disembodied
gods and when, eons on,
I swam the day away
in my Lake's billowing blue,
I thought I could hear the chime
of their chanting above the
lonesome bugle of a loon.

School Day
Sarnia Township: 1948

Morning in September,
the trek to school,
dust-puffs where our feet
fling, water welling
in the ditches, a tickle
of sound, on the fringes
goldenrod gleams, shaggy,
wind-shook, our lunch
pails swing with a
shrivelled squeak, girls
on their own side, winsome
and wary, bows in the
halo of their hair, winking,
skirts demure where the
knees knot, boys
boasting, scuffing stones
astray, too brave
to blush, somewhere
a heifer howls, pregnant
with pain, and there
where the schoolhouse
stands immaculate in its
pasture, the big-horned
bull bellows.

At Play
Point Edward: 1948

Night settles down
in soft surrender along
our stretch of the street,
aloft, stars define
the architecture of the dark,
the moon eludes a tug
of the tide, its glow giving
shape to shadows that seep
sideways, under, shudder
in the blood, boys and girls
at play where Mara's lamp
lingers light, gendered
bodies in summer's swelter
sweating sex, running
rogue from the thing
that breathes below the breath
towards the Bogeyman,
dancing with Death.

Dunes at Canatara

These dunes, older
than Methuselah's dam,
lie adrift in their own sleep,
crowned with sea-grasses
that weep in the on-shore
breeze like the wind-ruffled
whiskers of an aging saint,
and when as a boy I coveted
every inch of these summering
hummocks and lay bare-
bodied upon their hoarded
heat, I thought I could feel
the centuries flinch.

Blithe

For Katie and Rebecca

O my granddaughters!
Still in the budded bloom
of girlhood and all your lithe
loveliness, and I'd like to see you,
here and far into the new
century, groomed for greatness,
star-endued, blithe
in spirit, and I would call down
the angels from their lofty above
to keep you safe in their harbouring
arms, and when it's time,
sing your souls to sleep.

Adam's Dream

The grass on Grandfather's lawn
was as green as Adam's dream
of Eden and lilacs on the hedges
were licked livid by light
and leaves on the twinned maples
were embossed by the breeze and a robin,
bachelored in his shadow, with a song
throbbing in his throat, and I reconnoitred
my domain like a starved bard
in search of words to wield
the world anew, at ease
here, where love-and-loss
were yet to be born,
and I would loiter at the edge
of everything vivid and find
some inward glimpse
deemed indelible by the dawn.

Roan

Grace Leckie's roan,
ripe for rut, struts
into the bay's stall,
and while the boys bray
and the girls snigger, the big
stallion mounts the mare
and pulls the trigger, and we
are all in awe of such
a loveless clutch, such
a rude infusion in such
a bruising embrace.

When First I Set About

When first I set about
to venture verse, it issued
from some fissure in the blood,
a thought-not-yet-wrought,
girdled in words, a feeling
too raw to be believed,
caught in the mesh of a metaphor,
or a notion needing room
to breathe in the parameters
of a poem, and in our greed
to master meaning, we risk
oblivion, and bleed.

Swelter
Point Edward: August 1947

I remember the days when the
pavement puckered and the heat-
haze hovered above us like a
sun-muffling mist,
and roses on Mara's Lane,
to spite the swelter, bloomed
ambrosial and the leaves on Gran's
maples drooped in luckless
loops and the last of the lilacs
had long ago lavendered
aloft and all things
still greening wilted
in the sizzle, and we sweated out
the Summer on Canatara
like budding beach-bums
up to our hilts in the cool
jewel of the lake we loved.

Storied

For Anne in loving memory

I'd like to take you
by the hand and walk you
along the sands of Canatara
under a midnight moon
with breakers from our lake foaming
at our feet in fragile fury,
beside dunes older
than Adam's arrival in Eden,
shrouded in shadow or lit
by mellowing light, but you
have gone to your grave where only
the brave with their heathen hearts
abide, and I must stroll
these storied shores
alone, content to let
your soul breathe in my bones.

from:

Lover's Moon

Lover's Moon
Guelph: January 1961

For Anne in loving memory

That night snow hung
young in the air for a
breathless second before glistening
the grass with immaculate satisfaction,
and we ambled through the lazy
haze of fletched flakes
and their feathered frisson, our palms
overlapped like penitents in prayer,
as if we might be more
than merely friends, and anchored
there in the evening's ease,
knew somehow that,
above the cloud-clutter
a lover's moon loomed,
limned in sanctified light.

Bringing In the Sheaves

Coop and I: helping
the Leckies bring in the wheat,
me: teasing the reins
of sibling Clydes, guiding them
between the stooks and their weeping
sheaves, tipped up into
teepees to solicit the sunshine
and hoard its heat, and we rouse
a kildeer, skittering off
like a one-winged bandit
surprised with the loot, and a posse
of cowbirds, pecking at the spoils,
fling themselves skyward
in a flutter of feathers and avian
umbrage, and the afternoon
drifts on like a moon in slow
motion, and I want this day
and its summering serenity
to abide, and be.

Arrangement

My Dad built us a chicken-
coop with a wired pen,
then populated it
with a dozen barred rocks
and a single cockerel, king
of the grange, who hopped aboard
his harem of willing hens
whenever his kind of loving
was required, and the boys, with a knowing
nod, were awed by the jig
in his jollying, and the girls, assessing
the scene, scowled, as if
to say "Whose giggling
god concocted this
arrangement?"

Just-Born

My friend Coop invites me
to admire his just-born
kittens, and there they are:
tiger-striped puffs
of fluff like their dam
but for the one dipped
in ink, reminiscing some
fugitive bliss—unwinking
and adrift on their mother's
nippled breast, eyes
squeezed tight against
a world not quite ready
to welcome them, and I wonder
what feline dreams disturb
their deep-down sleep,
other than the burlap bag
Coop's Dad will use
to drown them?

As a Flame Defines the Dark

For Anne in loving memory

Your loss lies bitter
in the bone, but I have already
forgiven your abrupt embarkation
for the stars, your lonely going
where only the brave abide,
but I'll remember you
until the last sun
un-stuns or the universe
embers out, for you
were wine and wherewithal
to a parched heart and lit
in me the light of love,
as a flame defines the dark.

Unblinking

Coop and I take turns
flicking the reins, as if
we were muscular enough
to manhandle the matched
Percherons, plodding along
ahead of us, unaided
by our Georgic lore, between
the rows of stooked wheat
and their weeping sheaves they know
as well as the way to the barn
for the evening dose of oats,
and we circle the field in lazy
loops, while the afternoon
oozes on like a somnambulist's
snooze, and I let the reins
whisper across those
heaving haunches, and think
of the god who dreamed such
hallowed, paradisal days,
and launched me upright,
unblinking, into the
Summer sun.

This Day

This day, I turn
eighty-four, and even though
my old bones rebel
from time to time, and my heart
rappels half-a-beat
slower, and the weight of all
those unyielding years
hangs heavy on the mind,
I can find room for love
and its beneficent blooming
and a rhyme or two to keep
my muse amused and plumb
the fertile furrows of Parnassus
(where Truth kindles and condoles),
and most of all, after eight
decades of striving alive,
I can still feel summer
in my soul.

License

For Tom in loving memory

Just once again
I'd like to walk you thru
the Milkweed Meadow,
where butterflies ride
the brim of the breeze and milk-
weed pods debouch
in silken sleeves and a puff-
adder glides in the grass
with more than enough
panache and honey-bees
thrum from bloom to bloom,
hectic with nectar, and meadow-
larks sing in the midst
of their winging like divas
in debut, and down by the marsh,
marigolds glow like slow
suns and bullfrogs trumpet
with full-throated throbs
and cattails are brushed russet—
but you have gone to your grave
and I am alone in the care
of gods who gave us leave
to love with a license to despair.

When First I Thee Beheld

For Anne in loving memory

When first I thee beheld
with your blue-eyed, freckled
smile, I caught my breath
before it fled and whiled
my worth away, then beckoned you
aboard my borrowed heart,
where you have slept, unsorrowed,
since, and O, my love,
I'd trade a hundred lives
to have you brought aloft,
to hold you, thirsting, once
more in my adoring arms,
and let your tears rinse me
whole again.

Loving

When the phone rang with the news
of my grandfather's passing,
my Dad emerged from the bedroom,
the receiver hanging limp,
and for the first time
I realized a grown man
could cry, for his body
shook with a sobbing that rippled
somewhere in the bone,
and it seemed to me like a
great oak broken
in the seething of the breeze, or a willow
whipped witless by the wind
or a great grief unmuzzled,
and he gave me a look that said:
"This, son, is what sorrow is
and loving, does."

from:

The Home We Never Leave

The Home We Never Leave

It was a summer Saturday
when last I walked out upon
my town, silhouetted by the sun,
down Alexandra Ave,
under the Bridge with its gaunt
grey girders and cantilevered
leap above the blue
turbulence below, then across
the Marsh and its tufted, wind-
whetted rushes to the River
and its seething speed, around
the slow-dozing point to
Canatara's sylvan sands,
cradling the Lake and the
antediluvian dunes,
then drifting past the Slip,
where sailboats cantered
on their keels, and on to the
hedged edge of First Bush
and into its dappled depths,
where, here and there,
whenever a nugget of sunlight
leaked through the cullendered
canopy, a butterfly blinked
and a robin worried a worm,
and I was now arrived:
a circumnavigator
like Magellan or Drake, gallivanting
the globe—only to find
the home we never leave.

Double-Doing

The girls are doing double-
Dutch on the walk next
door: Bonnie and Sharon
twirling the ropes in looped
ellipses, like a limp-wristed
showboat loosing his lariat,
while the one in the middle
does a two-footed
trot to the fiddle in her head,
eyes shut tight
against the hypnotic thrum
of hemp on cement, and there is
something ferociously female,
exotic or stalking in the entranced
dance of ropes and repetition,
as if something in the doing
has come undone.

Girl-Next-Door

Shirley, the girl-next-
door, twirls her baton
like a manic drummer on a
May-Day parade
and, tucked taut into her
tunic, struts her stuff
in tufted, white-laced
boots, and when she pirouettes
like a budding ballerina,
and there is only thigh
where skirt ought to be,
something tugs that shouldn't,
but when she sends my way
the smile of friendly affection
she's smiled before, she's once
again my girl-next-door.

Wounded

For my father in loving memory

I longed so much to be
the athlete my father was,
and though the War left us
separate, he came alive
for me in the news-clippings
he kept of his hockey heroics
in a thumbed scrapbook
I perused, wild with pride,
and when the Muse and I
finally met, I wanted
to paste his exploits in the
permanence of a poem, but wars
end and warriors come home,
wounded, and all too
human.

A Memorable Flight

Or how I lost my license

For my father, William Ernest Charles Gutteridge, in loving memory

My Dad with his brand-new
pilot's license in his pocket
(a dream of his ever since
he pulled propellers for other
aviators and watched them soar
into glory) and a weakness for whisky
sits in an all-night
diner, high on the evening's
intake and boasting to the next
table of a Cessna 180
purring for him on the local
aerodrome, and would the young
buck there like to try
his luck, and off they go
effortlessly airborne, and Dad,
nodding off (and now
on cruise control) and comatose
on the stick, wakes up
just in time to smooth
into the boondocks of Hamilton,
grins and says to his hitch-
hiking friend (shocked
blue to the bone), "And that,
lad, is how it's done."

Unsaid

For Anne and for Tom, in loving memory

Benumbed by the thought of all
that I have lost, I summon up
scenes of childhood longagos
I can never fully retrieve,
but even a glimpse of those
innocent images brings them
flooding back: of a would-be
boy-bard, trawling
Grandfather's yard
for something akin to simile,
stirred by words that seethed
inside, bred in the bone
and sought solace in the tellings
no other tongue had yet
extolled, as if the poems
I would someday compose
with a wild beguiling, ought
to leave their best sense
unsaid.

My Big-Boned Boy

For Tom in loving memory

You were such a big-boned
bountiful boy with your
cinnamon locks and azure
eyes, and I remember the day
I saw you first on skates
with your gliding, sturdy strides
and the hockey-stick, like a fillip
of flotsam in your four-fingered
grip, and when your team
switched ends, you startled
the skeptics in the crowd (and me)
by bearing down on your own
goal like a locomotive
breathing steam and looking
for rails to ride, and brushing
aside the whoops and catcalls
and frantic defencemen and all
attempts to alter your craftful
cruising, and the move you made
on your stunned netminder
would have occasioned kudos
from Rocket Richard, and it is
memories like these that bless
and buoy whenever I think
of what the world lost
when you took yourself (and joy)
out of it.

Something Dies

With every line I write,
something in me dies
before it blooms, as the sun
must set before its shine
re-arrives or the moon
glower before it gleams
anew, as if whatever
we love consumes the lustre
that lit it, as if the words
I purge from the purgatory of the page
were born from our unembuable
blood and lost belonging, as if
there were no room in the bardic
womb for anything other
than doing and dying.

Unaltered

Seventy years on
and I can still recall
the kids who kindled delight
in my boyhood days:
Shirley, the girl-next-door,
who set my heart alight;
Butch, the big brother
I never had, who kept
the bullies at bay; Nancy,
who drifted through my dreams
like a lodestone of loveliness
and stirred in me visions
of Lancelot and graceful Gwen;
Wiz Withers, who dazzled
our gang with gizmos and gadgets
galore; and Jerry Mara,
who swam like Tarzan's twin
and simply let me be me;
and I hope to meet them all
in Heaven—unaltered.

Collision

For Anne in loving memory

In one small, windowed
room, with sunshine on the sill
by day and moonglow
blooming by night, we lay
as lovers have lain ever
since Adam took Eve
in bevelled embrace and bartered
Eden for other delights,
and in the misted aftermath
of our carnal collision, I brush
your brow with my pilgrim lips,
kiss your lids alight,
bend your breath to the brink
of mine, and revel in the bliss
our bodies engender.

from:

Trawling for Truths

Angling for God

In Sunday school, we sang
of Jesus calling the Apostles
to be fishers of men, and I pictured
Simon Peter, rod-
in-hand, casting a line
into the gulp of Galilee,
hooking the souls abandoned
there and hoisting them
Heavenward, and when our Savior
bade us follow, we did,
glad to be angling for God.

Chill

When Coop and I wade
into the Lake's chill
and let it grip hip-
high, every vessel
in our body stiffens, including
the one imploding below,
and later in the change-room
we share shy erections
(before the dreaded droop),
at ease in the other's company,
and hoping the girls next
door will have found the peep-
hole we worried there,
and like very much what
they see.

Summertime Stroll

For Sandy, again

We kissed but once, a brief
brushing of lip to lip,
more pucker than passion,
but ours was a hand-holding
romance as we strolled the summer-
time streets of our town,
and I was happy just
to have a girl like you:
blissful in the grip of her glance.

Steadfast

Gran's kitchen, Summer
or Winter, was a season of its own:
as cozy as a cocoon, cradling
a chrysalis, or a furred feline
dozing in a dream, and my Gran—
aproned and bemused, her smile
as mellow as a new-begotten
moon—was its royal resident,
and no matter how further
afield I roamed, in head
or heart, that numinous room
remained steadfast, a distant
nook I still call "home."

So Bright and So Fair

For Bob in loving memory

O brother! How I long
to be once again
in that wee womb of a room,
where we lay abed against
the nip of the night, no more
than a handspan or heartbeat
apart, and hear your voice
as high and lyric as a love-
struck castrati, singing
"In the Sweet By and By,"
and as the notes of your song
dwindle in the dark between us,
hope that when you gain
that mansion so bright and so fair,
you'll find it glorious there.

Gerry's Dad

Gerry's Dad was a tail-
gunner, blazing away
at Junkers and Messers from the
hub of his glass-bubble
and dodging bullets that buzzed
about him like blundering bees,
while mine, safe on the ground,
waited on runways to repair
the Spits and Mustangs that limped
inland, and by and by
when it came time to talk
about the War, not once
did Gerry boast of his Dad's
bravura, and I was happy
not having to lie.

Hurdy Gurdy
Point Edward: 1947

On the last dog day
of August, while I was still
hoping to make it to eleven,
Conklin's Show and Carnival
landed on our Lakeview lot—
with its Ferris Wheel like a
petrified web, spun
by a tidy spider, and its carousel,
pumping organ tunes
plump enough to rouse
the pampered ponies we rode on
like Roy or Hopalong, and its
Tilt-a-Whirl tilting us
till we wilted, and O
the midway with aromas of
flame-fried patties
and onion-sizzle and whiffs
of cotton candy—where,
for a nickel we could pick a number
on the clacking wheel and see
it spin for some other
lucky winner, or buy
a box of Cracker Jack
and munch it till the prize
arrived, or have our weight
guessed, alas, to the ounce,
and where, for a dime and little
wit, we could watch the fat
lady sit or the Siamese
sisters share a twisted
hip—but no single
scent or sight or sound
could match that full-fledged
feeling of a midway day,
churning, like a hurdy gurdy
in the heart.

Hopes

For Anne in loving memory

Your mother warned you
never to marry a teacher:
she had hopes for you other
than a chalk-jockey, cowering
in a classroom and brushing
dust from his second-hand
suit, and like Browning,
she believed a lad's reach
should exceed his grasp, but found
the ambit of my ambition a foot
shy of Heaven, but I
pursued you anyway
with poetry and roses, and eloped
with her hopes.

Dervish

For my father in loving memory

You could strum a ukulele
like someone from the Islands,
sing like Bing (and out-
hum him), shoot pool
for pocket-money before
you could vote, and even then,
ice was your element (I can
feel the bite of your blades
and their urgent, sturdy
striding), and you were the
hometown hero,
praised everywhere in print
and furred photos, the village
rink incubating fame
and raucous applause, and who
among your antic fans
cared that you failed Grade
Eight three times
when you could skate like a
Dervish on a dare and dipsy-
doodle like the Rocket with his brooding
brows, and O what disappointment
when you chose the Air Force
and war above the pros
and a cozy career, leaving me
(not yet three) to wonder
where you went and who
you might be.

When I Am Gone

When I am gone and the bones
which kept my body upright
and ept are feeding the flames
that will render me ash to furnish
an urn, the million million
thoughts I've distilled in the mnemonics
of my mind will float free
and fend for themselves
unless, as I often suppose,
they've found some solace in the
havened home of my poems.

from:

Kingdom Come

A Wide Berth

My Gran warned me that whenever
I was walking to the beach,
I should give a wide berth
to the odd, green, flat-
roofed abode with the steamed
windows, barred doors
and humped hedges, that Burch
explained, *sotto voce*,
was a Turkish bath, where men,
too nude not to be
noticed, had their bellies
rubbed, while squatting in tiled
tubs like Sultans to let
the heat swivel their sweat
and blister their body, and even
though I lurked and looked
a lot, the only soul
I ever saw leaving the premises
was a neatly-suited gentleman
with a Bible under his arm
and a worried smile on his face—
as if he might be late
for his meeting with God.

Harry Fisher

Harry Fisher, veteran
of the Somme and other killing
grounds, occupied a stucco-ed
abode on the corner of Monk
and Michigan, his yard—front,
side and back—littered
with failed fridges, castaway
ranges, old stoves,
staggering in the sun, abandoned
beds with coiled springs
the wind whistled through,
a three-legged couch,
leaking innards, a baby-
buggy with no infant to hug,
and sundry other pepper-
pots and gimcrack crockery,
and any afternoon saw
Harry pacing the Main,
in search of something he could never
quite find—in the clutter
of his home or the maelstrom of his mind.

Scraps

For my father in loving memory

When you failed Grade Eight
for the third time (all that
scrambled grammar and words
estranged on the page), you must have
thought the world didn't want you
in it, but you'd already found
your skating legs and a rink
big enough to take you
in stride, and here in the scrapbook
you kept for me to find,
your name leaps from headlines
in bold New Roman:
of goals scored and last-
minute winners and hat-trick
magic and trophies won
for the home-town fans—
and no-one cared you hadn't yet
read *War and Peace,* for you wrote
your own biography in the
blood and blade of your game.

Tea Service

Upstairs, tea was forbidden
fare, but below, where Gran
ruled the realm, tea was
taken with ceremonial flair
in bone-china cups
so thin you could see
you chin shimmering on the
other side, and O how I
loved its steaming, golden
glide from spout to the wee
splash of milk already
there, and two spoons
of sugar, sifting, to sweeten
the tooth, and what a joy
it was to be sipping on something
blissfully illicit, banned
above, and served with a
grin from Gran.

January Moon

For my mother in loving memory

You had just turned twenty
when you worried me into the world,
your wedding: hastily arranged
on foreign terrain, where a license
was easy on the dollar, your diamond:
a chip some gimcrack jeweller
jettisoned—and the young luminary
you worshipped from the moment you spied him
inkling in a rink and skating
like a bird in feathered flight,
barely old enough to vote,
but bathed in the raucous applause
of the hometown arbiters,
and you must have made love
under a January moon
in the star-harbouring dark,
but I bloomed too soon
in the womb, and so it was
we rode eight months
in tethered felicity, and when
I was born, you brushed my bard's
brow with your loving lips
and let me be me.

Jewel

For Tom in loving memory

You tried so hard to kick
your addiction, talking even
of someday taking your own
family to Cameron, and showing off
the lake where we spent so many
sun-numbed afternoons,
afloat and free to live
in our skin, and I was sure
that love, like the jewel that makes
the crown, would do the trick,
but you fooled us all—
you died.

Tuck

My father decides it's time
we try our luck angling
in Mitchell's Bay, where the fish
are as thick as Ali Baba's
thieves, and I am appointed
to guide our fifteen-foot
Peterborough and its purring
ten-horse Evinrude
along the meandering, back-
tracking Thames with a deadhead
threatening every bend,
and when we reach the river-
mouth, still afloat
and as tidy as a friar's tuck
(and I give myself a cheer),
the great weed-wracked
bay beckons, where jut-
jawed carnivores cruise
and connive, and here, my Dad
beside, with the sun in love
with light, I am glad to be young
and alive.

Heart-Healed
Point Edward: 1946

My Grandfather: on his "back forty,"
in the summer-softened sun,
his torso as bronzed as a Benini,
the sweat of his endeavour
burnishing his brow, and this
is the man who spent the green
years of his youth hunched
in the mud and mire of Flanders'
unpoppied fields
and its hand-dug, rain-
drenched trenches (where death
was less than a breath away),
and lived a terror-tugged
month on the Somme when thousands
went down before him to glorify
their king, and here he is:
long home from the Wars,
heart-healed and mowing
lawns.

Duo

For Anne in loving memory

I would not turn away
from love or the swerve of your smile,
even though I know
the chance we take whenever
we leave our hearts open
to hope and happiness, but we are
blood-and-bone beings,
eager to atone for the truancy
of touch, and break the back
of our aloneness—of the Muses.

Holy

In the midst of a May morning
I take my daily stroll,
my aging bones assuaged
by the subtleties of the sun, and everything
born to bloom is blooming
now: the serviceberry afloat
in its froth, the cupped loveliness
of a mauve magnolia,
cherry boughs hung
young with snow, forsythia
still thrilling, and the last
of the daffodils casting a golden
glow upon my inward eye,
and I wonder what I have done
in my indifferent decades
to deserve such immutable
beauty—with words enough
to keep it holy.

from:

A Goat-Footed Dance

Symphonic

I sit at ease in my rocker,
84 years young,
still able to breathe
in my bones, listening
to Peter, Paul and Mary
sing the songs of the long-
ago Sixties, that brought
the blood up and wakened us
to the world, or stung our cherub-
cheeks with tears that such
glorious chording, such
disarming harmonies,
such melodious musing
should be un-lunged
and bloom anew in our ears
like a seven-sea-ed symphony,
letting us know we are human
after all, and Heaven is nothing
but a fine-tuned heart.

Rules
Point Edward: 1946

My friend Butch, had a theory
that the snakes he killed (because
they let their venom drool
on his shoes) came back to life
at midnight, including the one
twisting in the grass ahead
he'd clubbed to oblivion with his fake
shillelagh, and we watched its skin
quiver and start to stiffen
in the cooling breeze, and as
my horror began to show,
Butch averred, "No worries,
the night will tell," but when
we returned the very next day,
the creature lay where we left it,
un-venomed and very much dead,
And Butch said with an indifferent
shrug, "Some garters
don't know the rules."

Wounds
Point Edward: 1945–48

A stone's throw from Grandfather's
house, I counted seven
alcoholics; *Charlie* next-door,
wounded by the War where it didn't
show till he'd downed a dozen
drafts; *Bob* over-the-road
unhappy with his lot, staggered
home to beat his wife;
young *Murph*, who sired
more kids he didn't want
and welcomed beer's oblivion;
tail-gunner *Bill*, who drank
to drive the heebie-jeebies
from his dreams; *Easten*, who found
more solace in booze than his
doldrum days in the grocery;
Ross around-the-corner
gutted by grief at the loss
of his toddler, sipped whiskey
till the pain drained; and *Harry*,
who still heard the big guns
above the Somme like an echo
only drink could deafen;
and how many more, unknown
to me, might have been,
swigging alone in empty
rooms to find courage enough
to curse the God that made them.

Dance Fancy
Point Edward: 1946

In those days, people
couldn't afford fancy
artisans from the City to paper
over a bedroom wall
or two, but Missus-Shannon-
across-the-road would nicely
do, and besides, she'd let us
watch her smooth manoeuvres
and brush-touch, and I loved
the way she unspooled the roll
along the treselled table,
as slick as a toad's tongue
tasting a fly, or applied the paste
in sluiced swoops with a besom
big enough to paint
a brigantine's bottom, and when
she reached the ceiling, and had
to stand without a wiggle
or a wobble, her down-
side up and flying blind
to keep the blooms aligned,
I waited for the smile that seemed
to say, "I don't dance fancy,
but I get the job done."

Chrysalids
Sarnia Township: 1951

Coop preferred the tractor,
riding its troubled clutch
with a tiptoe touch, and guiding
the hiccoughing hulk and its racked
wagon between the stooked
sheaves of ripened wheat
like a sure-footed chauffeur,
while I was partial to the taut
tug of the reins in my farmhand's
grip, and the gentle jigging
of the matched Percherons, who needed
no nudging to thread their way
through the sweat-whetted men,
tossing their tined bundles
aboard—and while Coop motored
and I moseyed, we were spun
lovely in the summer sun,
like chrysalids cocooned, as if
we might be freed from the
soulless cycle of the seasons.

Summer Sundays
Point Edward: 1947

Every Summer Sunday,
sun-shining Sabbath
or otherwise, Grandfather
marched a military mile
to keep his heart humming
and his blood in full flood,
and once in two blue
moons, I joined his parade,
stretching my strut to keep
in touch with his soldier's stride
and, arms swinging in rhythm,
we passed the cenotaph
where the names of long-ago
battles and the faithful fallen
are etched stalwart in stone
like a hieroglyphics of war
or the budded Braille of remembrance,
and we gave it a silent salute,
and walked on by the Slip
where sailboats dipped
their jibs into the witting wind,
and on it was to Canatara
and its drumlin-ed dunes, hewn
out of sand that Noah might've
poached for his beach-bloated
boat, and circling back
like pigeons drawn to the roost
that reared them, we addressed
the dappled dark of First Bush
and let its shadows have
their say, and soon found
ourselves home aboded
where I said a wordless prayer
to the gilded gods for the gift
of such a day.

Harvesting Heaven
Chatham, Ontario: 1953

I had just turned sixteen
as randy as a harlot in a harem,
with an itch to drive our two-
toned hardtop till the
whitewalls withered or the girls
weakened, and when my father
suggested I escort one of the
party-goers rocking
their socs in the rec-room
below, too liquored to be sick
I played chauffeur to milady,
a blowsy, bloated blonde
whose eyes were too glazed
to blink or bat their lashes,
and we sat side by side,
unthinking in the dark,
until, safely parked,
I was stunned to feel a pair
of female fingers slither
on my thigh, and though my id
was aroused, this was not
the way I planned to harvest
"Heaven," or turn seventeen.

Resurrection

It was so humid that Sabbath
when they rolled the stone away,
unbrushed as it was by any
condoling breeze, that the bees,
hung with honey, hovered
in their hives, and gave up
their buzz for the nip-of-nectar,
and Missus Bray's blooms,
sun-tugged tulip
or deep-rooted daisy,
droop, sympathetic
in the heathen heat, and when
the dark comes down,
she prays for a righteous rain,
and the Resurrection.

One More Time

The Prince of Poetry Reading
June 25th, 2022

The aging poet does not
pose behind a podium
to project some bardic bravado,
he is seated, rather, in his walker,
awkwardly, as if he can feel
his bones brooding in their sockets,
and, wincing at "prince,"
he gathers what remains of his versifying
voice, glances at the words
swimming on the page below,
and begins, one more time,
to recite the lines still
marauding in his mind, hoping
against hope to find
the reason behind his rhymes
or a condoning abode for his poems—
content, this day, to let
the erotic of applause be enough.

Ambling

For Tom in loving memory

You and I, ambling
the manicured meadows
of the local links, happy
just to be walking together
thru the amber-hued afternoon,
and whenever your drive feathers
a fairway, you give me
a grin, as if to say,
"Did I really do that again?"
and up ahead, on the beige
acre of the green, when your putt
is cradled by the cup, and I nod
my unsurprise, and it's days
like this when souls synthesize
that are a gift from the gods,
who've decided for once
to let their envy unabide.

from:

A Fine-Tuned Heart

The Ogle of My Eye

For Grace Leckie

Grace Leckie, the ogle
of my eye, spotting an auto
whizzing past the school,
would shout, "He's goin' to beat
sixty," and then mention
yet again that her brother,
old enough to drive
the family bus, could better
that by five and leave
the doubters in the dust—and I thought
of my Dad in our ancient 'Olds
that baulked at forty and coughed
to a stop, like a ruptured rhino,
but Grace had freckles that left me
wheezing at the knees, and I
could have listened all day
just to hear her spout,
with two licks of her luscious
lip, "He's goin' to beat sixty."

Max's Taxi
Sarnia Township: 1947–1949

For Max Laur: In Memoriam

When the winter chill dipped
below the 'old' zero
and school was still a gelid
mile away, we made straight
for the sisters Laur and Max's
taxi: half-a-ton
or so of shivering tin
that had to be cranked into
balky submission, and while
Bob sat smugly in back
between the girls and their giggles,
I rode shotgun, hunched
in the meagre heat of the engine's
judder, and waiting for the cold
crunch of gears and the first
grumpy chug of motorized
motion—and Max's triumphal
laugh that made it all worthwhile.

Barely Five

For Tim

You were barely five,
your blue eyes lit with the
lustre of just being new
in the now, and we played in the
sand-box I built
for you in the shade of the old
garage, like a couple of bumptious
pups, and whenever I soaked
enough sand to make
a moated casted, you smacked it
flat with a golden grin
that has lasted more than
thirty years and kept
the kid alive inside
the man.

Fancy-fed

Whenever I want my fancy
fed, I merely close
my eyes and dream of the day
when Coop, the gang and I
set out to find what lay
beyond the unmarred dark
of Bob Leckie's bush,
long forbidden terrain,
and I felt like LaSalle with his sights
on some Mississippi
in his mind, as we breeched the
tree-flumed gloom
and let its shadows shiver
the shade—and whistling a Natty
Bumppo tune, I led
my intrepid troops into the
sunshine on the other side,
rinsing a derelict windmill,
flapping its blades in the breeze,
and no-one among us
needed a map or illustrated
guide to tell us we'd found
ourselves a genuine buccaneer's
barque in full sail—
abloom in the boy-soil
of our mutual imagination.

Cossetted

Sarnia Township: 1949

The field behind our country
school was a lapsed pasture,
its sun-lashed grasses
corralled by a chicken-pen
fence, unbarbed and breeze
brushed, and we dallied there
in its ample ambit, as cosseted
as bunnies in their burrow, and O
how we sped when the wind
was a-lee, my rugby birthday
ball tossed from palm
to palm just to feel the ounce
in its bounce, and the girls galloping
with us, long-legged
in the flounce of their frocks—and there was
no-one to remind us that clocks
ticked and that our hickory-
docked world might come
undone.

Why

Sarnia Township: 1951

My dog, Moochie,
was a water spaniel with webbed
paws that offered him
locomotion, should he ever
find himself up to his ears
in a lake, but anything that ebbed
and flowed gave him pause,
even the twitch-grassed
ditch that bordered his bailiwick,
but once on the road and pebbled
underfoot, he assailed every
upstart auto that passed
his way, like a rebel with a cause,
conniving to clamp his doggy
jaws on the offending wheel
and its impudent whirl or stun it
still with the baleful baying
of his bark, and O how I recall
the misted mornings when he trailed us
to school a mile away, like a hound
on a hare's drool, and settled
himself on the sun-warmed
porch till a pooch-loving
pupil tossed him a crust
or half-eaten apple,
and I remember, too, the day
distemper struck, and his puzzled,
pleading eyes, and the afternoon
my father dropped him off
on some empty acre
of the countryside—wondering
where he was, and why.

Fuss

On Sunday summer evenings,
when the heat is heathen-deep,
the big front doors
of the Gospel Hall were flung
wide to let what little
breeze there was breathe
between the pews, and Gerry
and I, crouched beside
the stoop, listened in
to their Sabbath shenanigans,
hoping to hear them
talking-in-tongues some
biblical gibberish or Holy-
Roll up and down
the sanctified aisles—
just to please Jesus
or save their sinning souls,
but we wondered aloud if Heaven
itself was worth such a fuss.

Ukulele

I never wanted to play
the ukulele like my Dad,
or sing like Bing, crooning
to the moon, or be as cocky
as the "Rocket" glowering down
a goalie, or impress a freckled
face, or run away from home
to a Barnum-and-Bailey gig,
or keep the Sabbath holy,
but O how I yearned
to find the Why in the words
that trammeled frantic inside
like a Dionysian dirge
I might, someday, assuage
on the white bit of the page.

Thumbs

O to be that boy again!
to befuddle in puddles the rain
bequeaths and the sun shuns,
and feel their mud-luscious
shudder on our greedy, kneading
thumbs, and play away
the halcyon days at potsies
off-the-wall (cat's-eyes,
the prize) or jump-rope
till our pulses plump,
or bounce-a-ball to please
the girls and their awkward gawking,
or loping along in the wind's
ease, just to let
our feet find the secret
of their equilibrium and let
our breathing seethe inside
the stunned thunder of our lungs—
but—what once was
is always becoming, and joy,
however bright, is what's left
in the embers of our ripe
remembering.

Iceman

When I was six or seven
and Heaven awaited the faithful,
I wanted, when I grew big
enough for my britches, to be
an iceman, like the one who loped
lopsided down our walk
with a fifty-pound block,
tonged and tamed, in his five-
fingered grip, and I loved
the way the ice wobbled
with shards of sunlight shivering
inside, and got itself slung
up into the big kitchen—
box, where it dripped in the dark
to keep our goodies chilled,
as we raced to the truck, popped
slivers of chipped ice
onto our tongues, and let them
glide.

from:

A Ground More Arable

Body-and-Soul

I'd like to think that some-
where we are all immortal
in a place where the good gods
grin and forgive, where some
semblance of what we once were,
abides and breathes, a sanctuary
for the solace of souls, where we can
recall everything we've un-
remembered, and those we loved
till our bones bled and surrendered
to Death's dominion, bind up
our wounds, and even though
we may believe in Heaven's
leavening or the gift of its grace,
body-and-soul will find
a way to come uncoupled
and grieve on their own.

Tom-Foolery

For John

After a hard night's
partying, it was my turn
to make breakfast for my son,
and we sat together on the
chesterfield, staring at the
Abbott and Costello show
on our blurred black-and-white,
me: through my hangover haze
and you with wide-eyed
delight, as the comic duo
dazzled us with their "Who's on First?"
fandango—Abbott, like a slim,
mustachioed lothario,
delivering his impertinent ripostes
with Gatling-gun gusto,
while Costello, like an under-plumped
dumpling, parried them with jowled
bewilderment, and O how you
howled (when the giggles allowed)
at such divine drollery,
such cosmic tomfoolery.

Balm

Every evening when I was a
summer shy of seven,
before my bed could claim me
for sleep, I would slip downstairs
to say "sweet dreams"
to my Grandpa, and found him,
as ever, at ease in his soft-
bottomed rocker, the only
light in the room, that which
seeped in from the kitchen,
where Gran was counting stitches,
and the hunched console in the corner
with the orange throb in its throat
was pouring out the dreadful
news of the day, and I wondered
if his thoughts were drifting
towards the long-ago war
he'd weathered or the one on the radio,
where his sons now fought—
beyond the balm of his loving.

Gothic

In Leckie's barn, we feel
the hush of hay in manger
and mow, note the fluting
coo of pigeons somewhere
aloft and hear the breeze
of the milch-cows' breath
and the pleading bleat of a
newborn, on stilts in its stall,
and the resident owl, estranged
from light, rearranges
his scowl, and in the far
dark a bat unwraps,
and I think of cathedrals in their gothic
yaw and buttressed bellies,
and a place where prayers are soft
enough to be heard in Heaven.

Fandango
Point Edward: 1948

for Shirley McCord

Shirley does her fandango
on Grandfather's lawn,
her girl's body still
unbloomed, as lithe as a
willow bending in the breeze,
but in the hurly-burly
of her hips and the frantic prance
of her gams and the pelvic
pout of her lustrous lips
and the intimate glint her eyes
give out, something
of the woman's she's doomed
to be comes through—
a slow Venusian moon
igniting the sky.

Lingo

In the Point we had our own
lingo, not quite the lexicon
of Shakespeare or Winnie,
but rather our way of naming
the world that grew us
and kept us ept: and so
the local drinking den
was always the Bal-morale
and Barr's Billiards just the
pool hall and the bulrushing
marsh was just our mosquito-
breeding swamp and the woodlot
where we walked our Sundays
along was First Bush
just because it was
and the indiscreetly-heaped
garbage pits were just
Dunham's dump and the plinthed
Cenotaph was just the monument
on which kids gambolled when school
was not and the Blue Water
cantilevered beauty was just
the bridge and the Saharan sweep
of Canatara where silicone
tingled our toes was just
the beach and its Park just
a place for picnics among
the hundred-year oaks
and the City Golf Club
that sprawled obscenely green
across our borders was just
the lawn for doctors walking
their Wednesdays—and these
homely monikers and heartfelt
appellations were bestowed
with friendly affection and the
ballast of belonging.

Helter-Skelter

When summer storms rolled in
unthrottled from the throat
of our Great Lake, we dashed
outdoors, bathing-suited
and bare of foot, squelching
the saturate grass, paying
no heed to the rain's rage
or the wind's welter, for we
were young and far too
immortal to be bottled
or have our helter-skelter
ways succumbed.

Halo

For Anne in loving memory

Four years have passed
since last I wisped a wayward
curl from your brow or lingered
long upon your lips
or hugged you snug in my bravo-
embrace, and there was always
something holy in your soul,
un-martyred and merciful,
that left me aglow—with a
halo round my heart.

Below the Bridge

Point Edward: 1948

Down below the Bridge
in the bog, where bullfrogs
in the croaking throe of their throats
are making a rueful music
and bulrushes are brushed hirsute
by the breeze, and water-lilies
un-wizen in the sun and marsh
marigolds glow golden
and a bobolink sings, like a
minstrel on his lute, the syllables
of his name in rippling triplicate—
Butch and I pass merely
by without a nod or a wink
to the gods who dreamed this peaceable
place and let it be,
intent as we are in thrashing
the grasses agog in hopes
of startling a harmless garter
and watching it twitch away
like Lucifer exiting Eden,
and something in the soul
of this setting redeems
our casual passing and wakens us
to the ripe ritual of the day.

Stories

For my mother in loving memory

There were no books
in Grandfather's abode,
upstairs or down, but during
the War, when nights were long
in the curtained dark, my mother,
alone with two toddlers
and her thoughts, perused her way
through a shelf-and-a-half
of bloated tomes from our little
library (tucked above
the jail) before the nine
o'clock curfew shuttered
the town, and I watched her reading
from my invalid's bed, her lips
moving to the fictive rhythms
on the page, and I wondered, even then,
if the stories she inhaled
might heal the lesions of her loneliness.

Welter

During the War (I knew
only from the absence of the father
I was said to have somewhere
in the alien air beyond
my loving and lofting over
Labrador), I watched
my grandfather in tunic blue
and brass put his young
cadets through their paces
in the high school gym,
and never once did he glance up
at me and my adoring eyes,
and I wondered whether, in that
inner ear which never
leaves us, he could still hear
the hum of bombs, flung
in random rage above
the killing fields of the Somme,
and prayed those lads
would find some other way
to test their mettle or justify
their being than in the fratricidal
welter of war.

from:

Masters of the Craft

Note:
Masters of the Craft: second edition (published in 2021) is a small but energetic book, quite different in content from others used for this Selection. It is a kind of 'concept album', like those old rock records from years ago, *Sgt. Pepper*, *The Wall*, *The Dark Side of the Moon*, and such. Here, poem after poem, Gutteridge elegantly pays homage to a specific writer he has admired through the years, using sharp and allusive verse, always delivered with wit and glazed in a respectful awe. As John B. Lee says in his "Introduction" to the second edition: "These poems give us the poet as a reader of poems. They are each and every one something of an invitation to common admiration." While the whole collection is probably best read whole, what follows offers a creditable illustration of the poetic intent, a sampling of those writers Gutteridge honours as masters of their craft.

Hardy

You penned novels to make
a buck, not knowing
that *Jude the Obscure* wouldn't be,
or that guileless girls everywhere
would find in *Tess* and the dark
arc of its narrative something
to unease, and that
the bad luck in *The Mayor*
brokered by the Fates, would prompt
alarm in the Presbyterian
heart, and so too
do we have the poems, standing
in their own light, words
as chiselled as china, as sturdy
as star-struck Stonhenge—

Milton

He sang of man's first
disobedience and fruit
forbidden in the breezy demesnes
of Eden, like a purblind Homer,
in pentameters that pulsed
like thunder rumbling before rain,
and the Lucifer he drew soared
more flamboyant than the flawed
epicene angels around him,
whose God hemmed and hawed
while Paradise perished, and then,
as if to atone for such
irreverent ructions, he penned
the loping, lyrical lines
of *Lycidas* and its purring,
pastoral passion, and he left us
with the timeless sonnet of a man
resigned to waiting out
this dark world and wide.

McCrae

You bequeathed us a single
poem, that bloomed in the blood
and mud-mire of Belgium's
grim, marauded meadows,
a perfect rondeau of poppies
blowing crimson in the wind
between the groomed graves
of the patriot dead, and you bade us
keep faith with those
who fell in the gelded fields
of Flanders, and the timeless rhymes
of your lament will breathe again
in the embers of our remembering.

Browning

I first encountered him
and his "Epistle" in Senior
High, seated in the first
row, beneath the imposing
presence of Miss Stevens,
who read the poem aloud
to us as if she were averse
to the alien algorithms
of blank verse, until
she began to stutter upon
"gum tragacanth," and came
to a full stop, letting
the clotted consonants whistle
thru the gap in her incisors
a second before the spittle
followed suit, and she proceeded
to scrawl this arcane
locution across two
blackboards, and explicate
the length and width of its
encrypted syllables if
the poem itself had little
to do with the levitation
of Lazarus or the miraculous pizzaz
of Jesus or a front-seat
pupil, thumbed numb
by the poetry.

Wilde

He used his wit as a weapon,
a slim scimitar to expose
the foibles and follies of his fellows,
and mock their mincing hypocrisies,
and afternoons at Tite
Street saw the literati
and wannabees gather to watch
wisdom drip from the Great
Man's lip, or be a quarry
for one of his quips, or hear him
recite lines about erstwhile
Ernests or the lady with the
mishandled fan, and few
knew of his evenings on the prowl
for rent-boys with sordid
souls to appease a passion
for the love he dare not
name, and even the fury
of his fame could not save him
from the ruin of Reading Gaol,
and he perished a pauper in Paris,
unremembered even
by those once enlightened
by the laughter he lent them.

Eliot

When Prufrock with the bottoms
of his trousers rolled, hit
the pristine pages of *Poetry*,
he shook the panjandrums
of verse down to the shiver
of their shoes, and you caught
in the lassitude of those lines
something of the malaise
of those derelict days
before the horrors of war
made the blood-beat
of ballads impossible, and then
you stunned us once again
when *The Waste Land* tore
its scorched-earth truths
across our complacencies,
unrhymed and rhythmic-raw,
and like Ludwig you bowed out
with late quartets, a brooding
fugue of sound and sense
that left "Little Gidding"
to illume our language, while the
women come and go
talking of Michelangelo.

Don Gutteridge was born in Sarnia and raised in the nearby village of Point Edward. He taught High School English for seven years, later becoming a Professor in the Faculty of Education at Western University, where he is now Professor Emeritus. He has published seventy-six individual books and several anthologies of selected works, including poetry, fiction and scholarly essays in literary criticism and pedagogical theory and practice. He has published twenty-two novels, including the twelve-volume Marc Edwards mystery series and a YA fable, The Perilous Journey of Gavin the Great, and forty-three books of poetry, one of which, Coppermine, was short-listed for the 1973 Governor-General's Award. In 1970 he won the UWO President's Medal for the best periodical poem of that year, "Death at Quebec." Don lives quietly in London, Ontario.

Email: gutteridgedonald@gmail.com.